ABSTRACT OF THE WORLD

Poetry

Cheri Lee Helfenstein

Paperback ISBN: 978-1-945587-70-2
Library of Congress Control Number: 2021912058

1. poetry; 2. relationships; 3. peace; 4. nature

Book editing and design: Dancing Moon Press

Front Cover Artwork: Cheri Lee Helfenstein
          Watercolor and Ink - *Embracing Life*
Back Cover Artwork: Cheri Lee Helfenstein
          Oil Painting – *Dream with Me*

Poetry Section Art: Charcoal Drawings: Cheri Lee Helfenstein
          Dreams & Truth - *Efflorescence I*
          Nature & Nurture - *Efflorescence II*
          Fantasy & Reality - *Wild Grass*
          Ebb & Flow - *In the Beginning*
          Love & Loss - *Winged Seed*
          Life & Death - *The Mindful One*
          Art & Soul - *The Wizard One*

Author Photo: Diane Kulpinski

Manufactured in the United States of America

Dancing Moon Press
dancingmoonpress.com

Bend, Oregon
Lincoln City, Oregon

DANCING
MOON
PRESS

DEDICATION

for Franz
for Annelise and Wayne

I love you like the morning sun. Always.

'You have to be willing to give up the life you planned,
in order to live the life that's waiting for you.'
Joseph Campbell

'For the fire
in your own life.'
David Whyte

ACKNOWLEDGEMENTS

I'm grateful to the following publications for poems in this collection that were published as earlier versions:

Blank Slate - Fishtrap Anthology 2010, Matter and Spirit, Writers Gathering

For the Dead Dragonfly - Literary Harvest, Volume 5, 2012 Central Oregon Writers Guild

Flower is a Verb, Freezing Rain Cold, Off to the Languid Lagoon - Fly Amanita, The Stories we Came to Tell, Fall 2013, Writing Ranch

Song for Little Bird, Canyon Brothers - Beaujolais Nouveau, Winter 2013, Writing Ranch

Born Alone - An Afternoon at Miller's Landing, A Chapbook by The High Desert Sojourners 2014, Nature of Words

And with humble appreciation to the Top Secret Readers:
SAF, WMF, FHH, MDS, EW, CB, DB, NH, TP, RJ and CJ.

Contents

DREAMS & TRUTH

ABSTRACT OF THE WORLD

Early in my sleepiness, I'm half dreaming of people who are
        unknown to me, they're discussing my health
                a morning meal, my painting life and travels.
Next, my Doctor walks in to ask me about my DNA and
        how I intently need to choose to eat nourishing food
           meditate and get more exercise.

Deep in the dark night, I'm on a Jet plane, flying once again to Paris
        then tending to my Lavender shop
           and catching the TGV train to Avignon.
The aroma is so pungent I woke up sniffing the quiet air
        hearing wind gusts, trickling rain. Saw myself
            sipping a Mocha Breva at the covered outdoor café.

I yawn groggy, still thinking about Ursula K. Le Guin passing away
        all that she had to share. I see her face, her bright eyes.
            'Speaking the language of the night', I hear her words.
The absolute resolve and belief in what she knew to be true for her.
        I rise inspired, to embrace once again,
           the abstract of the world, the vastness of the sky.

VOICES OF THE INVISIBLE

The voice of a mystic, insensible to everyone
incapable of being seen, non-perceptible, disguised
and full to the brim with hidden whisperings.

They are microscopic in the views of ghostly secrets
as concealed hermetical, shrouded by supernatural
inconspicuous modalities.

The invisible human soul, written and otherwise
veiled, abstract voices and sounds that only animals
could hear, cloaked and clouded in the latent night.

Surreptitious, unapparent to all, withdrawn
and sequestered in a shadowy covert vapor
of a 13th century ephemeral vestibule.

RECLUSE

It's like a long road in ardent early spring
   where you meander quietly
   hearing the full moon rise
watching the sky slip away to the last breath of evening
   surrounded by open space, no people
   no cars, no interruptions
stillness at its highest state, a recluse longs for this.

What cannot be explained, existing only within the soul
   sometimes you're born with it
   others acquire it
escaping time after time from endless sensationalism
   let the misty rain fall brisk upon you
   and journey alone
solitude is calling you recluse, no need to resist.

ZEPHYR

The huge double rainbow
fills the gray green heavens
more beautiful than words
        a welcomed phenomenon as
        Winter prepares to shed her blanket.

We cultivate our warmth from within
to embrace the frozen azure sky
soft sunshine cast in late afternoon
        shadows fall between stark trees
        fire red twigs and dried bushes.

Our thoughts are awakened by the
quiet beauty of seasons interchanging
warm to cool to cold wind morphs quickly
        whisking the breathing heart away
        as the Zephyr is slowly fading.

LIKE BLOOD

Below the misty surface, under the gritty dirt
seeking the light, climbing strong and determined
what seed can triumph, what root can dig in, then down
dense into Mother Earth where pathways nourish from all
Grand Dad trees of the ancient old growth, extending energy
to guide the young fledglings to live, to mature, to flourish.

Under the forest canopy where crystal sunbeams are scarce
there lives a mingled kinship of magic, secretly, quietly embracing
each tree large or small, each bush healthy or frail, all emergent as part
of one large earthly floor, each species connected yet with no constraint
gripped by nature, a family in co-habitation, with honor and celebration
the understory remaining strong, dedicated to its destiny.

Like blood, running through the veins of humans.

CONDITIONED

Women and men conditioned, some more than others
        many radically so, with narrow positions in society
yet fiercely imbedded in the marrow of the bones
        ostensibly handed down through DNA and blood line.

 In later years, the monster creeps, seeps
        through glassy eyes, and rotting hearts of cycles
repeated over and over, without reaching beyond
        what was said to be true. But it's not true, not even close.

Children conditioned, little girls and boys, in wonder
        how could this be, they ponder for years in the making
all is told with such conviction, hormones run, ebb and fall
        to either bolster further confusion, or mop the mind with doubt.

Escape is difficult, perhaps searching for it months to years
        listen for the internal blessings of who you might really be
if you discover it, you have reconciled with your spirit, all ages
        unbind the soul, to encompass ones' own cultivated life.

THE GREAT OBSERVERS

They're everywhere
usually no more than four feet tall
  trying to learn the alphabet
  flirting with the idea of reading.

Always told to go out and play
no matter the state of the weather
  as they observe deeply, all that surrounds
  them, externally and internally.

Eyes that see, ears that burn
so much they truly do understand
  little hearts pumping, shifting, breaking
  making it precariously through each day.

Innocent bantam kids of ominous capacity
kissing, hugging, forgiving, crying, running away
  knowing not to judge, or place blame
  yet hold tight the legacy of being the Great Observers.

I SHALL NOT

I shall not apologize for speaking my truth
small gestures exploded in my mind
  a glance, looking away, sketching
  a smirk, an uncomfortable laugh
all under the cordial sky of summer.

I shall not apologize for speaking my truth
but could not abide the rules of the trade
  never in the past, nor in the present
  unable to sit in a peaceful state
my body held tight, a quiet wrath.

I shall not apologize for speaking my truth
for even though uncomfortable
  it is, in itself, a known abyss
  to either chew the wiggly worm
or swallow the damn apocalypse.

THE QUOTE

There is no daylight for living our obsessions
determination or perfection encircle to stoke the flame
all the irony for latent imagination drives persistence inward
where people resonate with the obscure, ambition and emotion.

Cool jaded eyes never sleep with image dreams in the night
strange facial features on faces that don't match up
living somewhere between sheer anxiety and
a world pandemic, among social unrest.

Finding ourselves in an aggregate fantasy driven
existence, a dream world in which to escape.
Quote: 'Even amidst fierce flames…
the Golden Lotus can be planted.'

Author Unknown.

In memory of Sylvia Plath Hughes   1932 – 1963
The two line 'Quote' is carved in Sylvia's tombstone, Author Unknown

FLOWER IS A VERB

Stagger around the lit candle
walk briskly to the fork in the road
limp across the room and apply lipstick
run as fast as you can to find your favorite book
crawl back and pick up the cup of coffee you left behind.

Hop down to the corner café and order the lunch plate special
ride your bike to the hilltop school yard, quietly lose your shoes
fly high on the track field and sit still in the antique eighth grade chair
drive fast in the old Willys' jeep, steal your friends
go to the top of Table Rock.

Careen downhill on a wooden sled
cross the road lit by the cherry-pot lamp
reel to the flower box, wobble under a flying bird cloud
weave till you locate the sweet scent of ginger, then
sway with the flow of the river on a stand up boogy board.

Waver slightly aloof until you discover a true blue sky
sprint down the hours and daydream out the window
transport yourself through the opened secret door
take a trip to the other side of the world
bathe in the fervent lake.

Drift over the sparkling green Mediterranean Sea
breathe in the sweetness of life, rest on its benevolent shore
flower is a verb, though sometimes a noun
swimming in a guzzle of words.
Who knew!

Stagger around the lit candle
walk briskly to the fork in the road.

SPRING

Seems hopeful.
Standing in the yard
on a beautiful sunny day.
A large bellied red Robin
plopped down in front of me.
Looking me up and down inquisitively.
I stood very quiet. Having a hose in my hand,
water sprinkling softly onto the Crab Apple tree.

I must have looked like a watering receptacle
as the Robin just watched me intently.
About two or three minutes went by.
I decided that if I just stand still
and not move, that this
could go on for
quite some
time.

And it did!

NATURE & NURTURE

THE SCATHING UTOPIAN SKY

Florets that smile, seeds cried
a garden found and embraced
a happy home of embodied earth
began and ended on the front porch.

The country refused to listen
while Jupiter and Mars replied
'Hell hath returned and left again
in the scathing utopian sky.'

A Haven is believed to have been
accepted, by the King and Queen of
the Arctic Circle, all brothers and sisters
have heard the message, yet

this unique loft of laughter, looked
to be run by a rare jumping bean
sadly recited, over and over, but
nobody knows… what it means.

CURVE OF THE EARTH

As the meteor passes by, at the size of a small planet,
careening 26,000 miles away from Earth, as long as
it doesn't get knocked out of orbit by
other rowdy shooting meteorites.

We sit quiet and safe by the Pacific Ocean gazing
longingly out to the curve of the Earth
as the skyline disappears softly over
the thin perimeter, uninterrupted.

The ocean waves keep their rhythm
of tide in and tide out. Seagulls fly swift,
skipping the waters edge, dodging gusts of salty
sea sprays, with all things presumed in balance.

It's just a hint of time, a moment to reflect. There are
no voices, no stories to track, just that constant fervor
of the earth's thundering heart. Catastrophe diverts itself
one more time, in a huge pool of numerous possibilities.

On that, we tap into the constant rhythm of our own beating hearts
to embrace infinity and lift up our senses to the great mysteries
of the Earth, ocean and sky. Knowing in that second,
that moment, our only purpose, is to live a good life.

WHATEVER WE BELIEVE

From thick fog to soft mist
   clear sky to crumbles of sunshine
   grains of atmosphere to dark waves of nothingness
   changing glittering stars to bright forming constellations,

from the white light that calls us forward to whatever we believe is there
   we patiently await, the wisdom of providence.

Between fierce winds and silver cotton candy clouds
   roof tops, deep valleys and majestic mountain terrains
   a long arduous journey into the blissful realm of eternity
   vast horizontal existence and something no one can truly explain,

between a vision that summons or divine intervention of spiritual existence
   we patiently await, our foresight and our fate.

OF THE UNKNOWN

I observed my fathers' stoic life in awe and sometimes in anger.
As his anger became my own. His joy was slight and fleeting,
his striving to excel and go beyond, intoxicating.

I don't think I would have known this sweet lingering connection to nature
had it not been for him. We climbed mountains to heights that many
of my young friends had never known or would ever experience.

The gaze of the remote and vast grew me into worldly endeavors
and my fathers' quiet purr of longing catapulted everything into my own
personal version of the unknown.   I had not asked myself the question
of why I must go away to such far off places until now.

Why, as a young woman, had I gone head on into the dangers
of the unknown, often alone. In those days I knew I was not afraid
and could feel the astir strength alive within me. A fathers' strength,
the quiet purr I was born with, and the slippery slope of the unknown.

ONE INCREDIBLY LONELY DUCK

Blackbirds rode on the tail of the wind
and followed us over the Cascade pass.
        Beyond the Liberty Bell mountain
        and the Eagle and Black Bear Trail.

They fly-in squawking, together peck around
still squawking, then slip quietly into the hallow
        of a giant ancient Willow tree
        to sleep the night into day.

I'm transfixed by their character, long migrations,
and set patterns, as they stay in a very tight group.
        There is so much about life and nature
        that I really don't understand.

But a week later, on a warm fall day, with only
one single duck waddling around and around our camp
        do I finally understand, just how
        incredibly lonely, my Mother had always been.

CANYON BROTHERS

Wedged foreheads, square structure,
eyes… deep like canyons.
The stories they could tell as their souls
cry, from years of deterioration
not just torn by sun and wind but by
hiding deep, deep within the caves
dark and dripping tears
never shared just swallowed
over and over again with the rising river
and the swirling red rock sludge
gripping the gritty mud.

Sister creek beds wept torrents
tried to console but could not
calm the current, too fast
to tell the truth that blood
holds, increasingly crusted like
scarlet ruby moss, cascading down
solid boulders, stacked too high to climb over.
Years passed, sticky soil eroded, gravel
to sand, just as though no hillside path
had once prevailed, shifted earth, groomed
and open, as forgiving nature cracks.

Then death encroached upon
that frayed adventure, exposing
harsh weather patterns of the
undying truth. The canyon brothers
crumbled, one upon the other, with
no absolution to embrace.
Sister creek beds lost, abandoned
stubbles left of broken trees
absent now of desert creatures
no lofty place for birds to waver
or sing sweet songs... of peace.

SNOW DAY

I felt the sunlight on the quiet
             its weight a startling cold
snowed in for eternity sake
             imprisoned unable to go
anywhere, close by or far
             faced with what is right in front of
who we are and what we witness
             memories of a broken moment in time.

There was a word I couldn't use
             and then I forgot it.
There was a love I couldn't feel
             then sorely, I lost it.
There was a snowy day that held on
             what seemed forever.
And there was a sadness in my heart,
             that I knew would never go away.

NOT TO CRY

I don't know why but I couldn't
fathom what this dream could mean.
Mysteriously, the main details escape me.

Days out of sequence, first I am old, then
I'm young, little still with tiny wrists,
and lanky, willowy bird legs.

Stairways narrow, my sister holds my hand.
We take each step up very slowly.
She tells me 'not to cry'.

My brothers' voice echoes, in a whisper
'not to cry', but I cry quiet anyway.
Weeping hot tears down cool cheeks.

My siblings have come to save me.
Then suddenly, radiant flowers
on the front porch... appear.

RUNNING WITH LARRY

My brother Larry could make magic
out of sticks, light cloth and crepe paper.
He fashioned an unusual kite named Patches,
that could fly almost a mile south east of our home,
taken by the swift winds that barreled down the Columbia River.

I remember the brisk summer breeze that would rustle my hair
and flap my cotton clothes, as I stood sentinel down wind,
just to watch Patches fly. Larry kept extra string, to quickly attach,
so Patches could travel as high and far as possible. Incredibly,
floating over the fields of our little farm, and then above the highway,

where we were forbidden to go. Next, suspended and drifting,
beyond the banks adjacent to the mighty Columbia River.
I still see Larry running and abruptly stopping, watching in awe.
He would glance over at me to make sure his little sis was safe.
Then belly-laugh out loud, with a vivid glimmer in his eyes.

We would stay out until the sun began to set in the Wenatchee Valley hills,
small light beams appeared from the cars driving fast down the highway.
We could smell the pungent earth, the sweet sage, with cool evening air.
Flying Patches far beyond our forbidden zone of which we safely ventured.
Standing on the knoll, I felt as though, we might always be there together.

Larry has since passed away, and with him a special kind of enchantment. Without a doubt, we experienced a number of meaningful moments growing up together, yet this was the most fantastic, boundless adventure. Burned into my psyche for eternity; spirited wind, echoing laughter, vibrant excitement. Flying Patches, a primitive, beautiful creation. Making magic, and running with Larry.

SINEWY, FLOATING ASHES

Sometimes ashes should be dumped into veggie gardens
      for earthly amendment of the soil, but I'll take these ashes
      7 hours to the north, 25 miles up the lake, to the end of the road.

I'll drive them to a place where we played as children, when
      Mother was full of life and nobody had issues over money, or
      years of evolving through looming changes of the status quo.

When only the deepest love of a Mother and Son ensued
      where laughter was served up along playful games, and
      camping under an all-encompassing star lit sky.

I'll scatter their ashes into the water, the Mother and the Son
      together. Right where 25 Mile Creek spills its thunder into
      Lake Chelan, the deepest natural lake in the Northwest.

They can sail out together into that lovely, dark and mysterious
      body of water. Sinewy, floating ashes on top of the candescent
      clear blue green. Never to misunderstand, never to break a heart.

Ever again.

HUMILITY

We didn't launch the boat
we didn't like the cold wind and rainy season
we loved our brothers and sisters terribly
      strong but couldn't weather every storm.

Every change in tempo, every surge
from right to left, to who knew the real answers
who could persevere, who could not
      cry in pain from long ago. It's all over

we say, now is the time to accept
let the grief wash over. Travel that
long road to forgiveness, and recover
      sweep it off, shake it down, toss it to the wind.

I don't give a damn what anybody says
our Mother loved us equally, in her own
caged up way. Her own glorious
      life of fiction and fantasy.

We didn't launch the boat but
we continue to brave the stormy sea
every time her name comes up,
      we relive a good birth within humility.

THE BUTTERFLY MONARCH

I know where the Monarch flies
       and lives a life of freedom.
So serene I must confess
       I've never seen so many.

High up on a ridge,
       above the Stehekin Valley.
And all along the river beds
       softly gliding to Lake Chelan.

With cool breezes and open sunshine
       there is no encumbrance.
Nothing toxic to hurt them
       as they joyfully sail in the wind.

My spirit was lifted immediately
       my heart felt oddly unburdened.
A twist of fate, I will always cherish,
       to see the Monarch vibrant and at play.

ROCK ISLAND ROAD HOUSE

Remember how I loved you dearly
      your large slumbering porch across the whole front
      of the house. Fresh white paint, big windows, lots of light.
      Even the brick walkway and tended yard were so inviting
      an endearing scent of blue iris and red roses in our English garden.

Sun beams often drifted down to caress you while cool breezes
zipped through your rafters. I could sit soft on that porch
for hours and watch the entire world pass us by.

I felt free there, unencumbered
      safe in our sleepy neighborhood. Outside was ideal
      for adventure, as the gardens continued around the house
      into the allure of the back yard, something very enchanting about
      your big trees, and how tall they were, surrounding you like a fine estate.

A natural sanctuary away from the ever evolving universe.
No one could see you from the road. No one could see anything.
Yet you were there, remotely invisible. I loved you then, I still love you now.

I loved you dearly… remember?

FANTASY & REALITY

OFF TO THE LANGUID LAGOON

Sit slight in the poetic yet slumberous meadow, waxed
lyrical by its natural warmth and peaceful existence.
>Criss-crossed by the rusty florid fox, danced upon
>by the Butterfly Monarch. Deeply dappled with magenta
>sapphire and golden flowers in their various stages of maturity.

The color of the sun a fulvous reflection of reddish yellow
cast down over the literary lea mead. There is always a story
>to broadcast over the wild field of fancy, times of long gone by
>rendered from a memory bank, tossed to the wind from heart to
>heart, lapped up like a cool drink of water near the emerald shore.

As the stream serpentines through the terra firma, destined for
wondrous, viable, sweet perfume, we are off to the languid lagoon.

SAKURA RIDGE

A sea of emerald green within a gazing eye
beyond the mist of the atmosphere perspective.
The moon seven eighths full, not quite round, spills
a bright shimmer over the cool valley
                    and rising Mount Hood.

What is the universal truth, nothing personal they say,
with all things cast beyond the dark shadow of the moon.
The beating heart can rest here, fleeting sounds to contemplate
only the flapping of occasional bat wings
                    and a distant sprinkler.

Small planes take off from the fielded airport below. Little lights
change intensity as the pinions transport and lift to the darkening sky.
How long has it been since you fell asleep in the lull of the rocking chair
so serenely placed for the unequivocal lure
                    of an expanded, inviting porch.

Toward the end of a beautiful day, I watch the stars slowly converge.
The entire sky in a luminous display of radiant life and soft movement.
A wistful sigh of soothing wind, held notion to heal my tempered soul.
The absolute truth is the universal truth.
                    It is the tidal rise of the human spirit.

SONG FOR LITTLE BIRD

The solid knot of the tree
shaped like a little bird, fits in my hand
and speaks to me of an ancient discovery,
> then sends me right back to the moment rapt
> in the Grand Canyon with its roaring Colorado River.

There was a wink of peace as we stopped on the river bank
just before the next set of white water rapids. Here, the eddy
swirls with washed up driftwood of all shapes and sizes.
> Blissfully my mind is taken away from what lies ahead
> when running a river medley in the wooden dory.

It is a savory seasonal song that suddenly crescendos
and then falls back to the cadence of sweet pianissimo
back and forth, loud then soft, back and forth, loud then soft.
> I've decided to keep the little bird in my pocket for good luck.
> Haste, we load once again, precariously, back into the boats.

SOUL AND HEAVEN SENT

Little French girls, with sunny faces, at the Saturday Ganges Market
taking turns playing the violin, for grateful donations.

Then a tall French tourist talking fast, laughing out loud
waving his expressive hands all around in the air.

And the French baker with her soft blue-pearl eyes, smiling
sweetly, while speaking very rich Francais to me.

I dreamed I was in the sunny South of France again
sitting under large shady plane trees.

That my artsy French sisters were going to walk around the corner
any minute, to sit down next to me.

I contemplated painting in vivid colors this day, to capture
the mood, the temperature, the soothing light.

Watching hippy chicks with their hippy dudes dancing
barefoot rhythms on the prickly grass.

Listening to music playing, sassy silvery, melodic tunes
all at once with guitars and drums beating.

Comprising strong feelings of peaceful joy and common
ground among all the different, traveling people.

Finally, I stopped thinking, dreaming and just sat there
      enjoying this unique and serene moment.

I thought I was on a small, remote island in BC, Canada
      where people live a fairly simple, bountiful, happy life.

When all of a sudden I remembered, for soul and heaven sent
      that is, where I am.

THE LILT OF THE TURQUOISE SEA

She chants a periwinkle song, on a lavender clear day
where childhood memories skipped in and out of restful sleep.

The scent of vanilla shakes her back to a time before
a young woman danced her dreams alone, like a bluefish in clear water.

The Turquoise Sea, soft and lilting, will trill her name
until she rewrites the future, reminiscent of ambitious times.

The luscious body of water becomes a warm soft blanket
to quietly soothe her brittle bones in winter. From thousands of miles

away… she lives in its salty sweet air, and drinks
of minty aqua that surrounds her. In early morning, at just sunrise

she wanders the vacant beach in search of shells, pebbles
the afternoon muse, paintings of violets, rosemary and sage

to deeply imagine and re-enter there.
Captured facile by the lilt of the Turquoise Sea.

FETTLE LIPS

The kiss of Cirrus clouds
quiets the luminous viridian sky
lifting the anguish from my downward heart.

Not the usual look of clouds
but shapes like white fettle lips
stacked one upon the other.

Continuous, beautiful configurations
of minute ice crystals at high altitude
as they sally beyond the eastern horizon.

So mesmerizing, so fantastical
I could not look away.

THE OBJECT, PURE AND ABSOLUTE

The object of desire pangs, pulls
        slips to obscurity
                floats in a cloudy dream.
Simplicity of existence sleeps
        so benign it smells sweet
                born lofty in a life of calm.

Yet here, subconscious sets the gamble afoot
        organizes the list of players, plots
                suspended conclusions.
Wake each day with laughter
        vibrant quaking power
                pounding down a heartbeat.

Skate through a brain warp
        foraging strength of a stoic mind
                a beckoning intrinsic soul.
Look beyond open sullen eyes
        for an object spilling with desire
                pure and absolute.

Prone to waiting,
        seeking to be found.

THE DEAD DRAGONFLY

My heart weeps for the dead dragonfly
cast off on a lonely kitchen shelf
laid upside down, separate, lifeless
cracked wings, slowly drying, quiet.

I did Tai Chi in the kitchen this morning
and tried to avoid looking in its direction
yet 'soft gaze, soft smile' and then there
on the shelf that poor dragonfly... dead.

My heart weeps for that dead dragonfly
as life pulses onward all around me bright
cyan skies, soft breezes, butterflies dancing
on leaves of nasturtiums and tomato plants.

Ironically, the bird feeder just outside the
kitchen window hosts the little hummingbirds
in the early morn. I wonder if they too see the
dragonfly so close to their nomadic wanderings.

And weep and cry and feed and weep again
as they buzz away, full of life, bounding spirit.
Yet still, nothing can be done, as deep in my heart,
I weep, I cry and weep again, for the dead dragonfly.

THE GHOST OF EVERYDAY

A slender young woman with long blonde hair
bicycles up to the Steelhead Park, right
      to the second table in the picnic grove, right
      by the Skagit River, glistening with cool
      aqua green glacier-like water.

I don't see her until she enters the tree line
walking slow to lean her bike on the end
      of the picnic table, unties her golden hair pony tail
      shakes it out in the sun, drops her sweater on the table
      walks even slower to the river.

Then, I never see her after that, but only seconds later
I look up and notice, the bicycle is gone from the table
      no sweater, no young woman, no sound, no sign of her
      and nothing beyond the furthest tree line.
      Everyday @ 12:21… she's just gone!

THE SKAGIT

A tribal name for this mesmerizing river
>   that shimmers in the sun and changes color
>   from sandy to river green, and then to ultramarine.

Tall deciduous trees shade the glen
>   up to the beaches while leaves carry a most
>   warm, peaceful, rhythmic vibration.

The valley whispers within Cascade Mountains that soar
>   a river that moves swiftly to the sea, but not
>   too fast, as nothing here is ever hurried.

This is how we all should live. Governed only by
>   morning sun, the wind and dusk to sleepy night
>   yet all things connected by a mind that is freed.

I know what the Skagit is telling me, if only
>   I will listen. My life isn't someplace else. My life
>   is within me, wherever I am. Beautiful and unfettered.

STORM TEMPEST

The lichen measured slowly
>to the sand
Hammered rock
>to scree

Moss on the snag screwed inward
>to the core
Hung, cut, leveled and split
>to the wind

A howl above, a feather sinks soft
>to the ground
Oh river wide, raucous through, drill down
>to the sea

Lightning stacks, nails the trees
>to infinity
again and again.
>This never, ever stops.

EBB & FLOW

DRAGON HEALER

The Fire Serpent shifts and bobs
sending chi to heal the wounds.
Years of weaving, breathing deep
finding reasons to live again.

Wander soft into the wisdom
reading beauty locked in books.
Forgiveness shrouded in sweet
feelings, pulsing true the heart.

Once closed, unfolds to open,
wrap and ping, Fire Serpent.
Weave the Dragon, as it is so
knowingly, ready to be done.

SOMATICS

There was no sky
        Just black and white gray
            All that you love
All that you like, bring it on
        Somedays you just have to
            Take yourself away from
All who are oppressed
        All who are traumatized
            By where we live or who
                Governs.
So when asked
        What's in your visceral
            Gut, can you
                Spill it out
Onto the floor
        Grimace, scream, cry
            Can you poop it out, like a
                Bad dinner of uncooked pork
 How much can you
        Shock, offend, or tap into
            That sad and jaded heart
What's in your body, so solid
        That you just can't
            Get it out.

Is it hatred, disgust
      Unfairness thrust
         Upon you
Was it early on
      In your life
         Stuck at Auto-repeat
Over and over again
      Like a bad, bad
         Dream, that
You know not
      Literally
         How to escape.
To relive in sequence, yet
      Somatics can be mysteriously joy, or
         Sorrow, distilled hatred or
Blissful reaching, out beyond
      The pain of the prison
         Within
So now I ask you this...
      Do you prefer somatic rage or
         that somatic visceral love of life?

BORN ALONE

I was born alone, like this river
      like this shore
            like this land.

Stewards come and go
      but who will care for us until the end
          until our death.

I feel more alive here
      standing among the pines
          near the river.

I can see the lifeblood
      of past and present times
          flowing by, in this river.

How many others stood here
      cried their tears, kissed their lovers
          or took their last breath.

We all live and die, with this river.

BLANK SLATE

Hiding behind doors and chairs
six years old and watching the days of washed out sky
knowing the same fragrances still, of the house, the yard
apricot trees, honey bees, chickens clucking, fresh cut grass.

A blank slate that no one knew
intertwined with moments of joy and simple pleasures
bright lights and loud music, a carnival of confusion and fear.
Can't get it back, can't let it go, it was always beauty, wrapped in disdain.

SAGACITY

The profound wisdom of a little boy before he is about to die
goes far beyond the knowledge of grown-ups asking questions.
What do we know of life when we are about to leave it
lose it, lose our grasp and our will to live
let go of the pain, let go of all that we love.

The courage of a little boy, forever held within his dark brown eyes
perfect until transformed by something foreign that will not be cured.
We know nothing of this life until it is about to be taken from us
only then do we know everything. The incredible depth of true love
wrapped in the memory of a single precious moment.

Holding tight to what matters most
a loving family, people who soulfully care.
Laughter, a summer breeze, the familiar scent of home
the sweetness, the innocence of just being a healthy child
the unforgettable sagacity, of a beautiful little boy.

In memory of Kaden Erickson

IN RETROSPECT

Life seems to be epigrammatic, brief, transient yet

How beautiful you were as a young vibrant woman, with a
lonesome smile and eyes like pools of McKenzie River green.
You loved to bolt upright when watching the world pass by.

In what conscious way do we release our intellect into the cosmos.

Hopefully, there are no regrets, having lived all the possibilities,
having faced each day with pride and respect for one another.
Having never forgotten what it means to hold tight a friend for life.

Always in retrospect, I believe you knew, how much I loved you.

ALIVE AND PRESENT

The eyes of the Buddha statue seemed open for a moment
as the melted snow and dripping water fell like darkened eyes
wide open, to see his placement within our garden, brief
yet remotely profound, as I looked into the eyes of Buddha
for the very first time.

In all the years we have possessed this peaceful statue
the eyes have been closed, serene, meditating.
I had no idea that melting snow as trickling water
could change all that, change the light to dark coloration
 of the stone, to free his calm, quiet, mysterious eyes.

I think I see a turned up twist to the lips, as a slow smile
comes and goes, at which still dripping water rambles
attentively down the full face of Buddha. Dozens of wild
birds are puffed up in the trees, while crisp white April snow
falls like lace, in meandering synchronized silent motion.

The leafy bamboo behind the now once again
sleeping Buddha, is bobbing down with the
weight of melting snow in a cooling breeze.
Buddha senses all movement; wind, fire, rain and
the changing status of our evolving simmering earth.

Perhaps the lesson is in stillness and observation.
To wake our sleeping eyes as well, perceiving truth
even if it isn't favored, desired or anticipated.
To accept things as they are and then move forward.
To fully acknowledge the beauty, laughter and love in life.

The sleeping Buddha always appears to be so wise.
We can only guess he knows all, in his own stillness,
his silent meditation, his solid concrete sleep. Until
snow dapples down once again, to open the eyes of Buddha,
animate his spirit, observe briefly, then gaze directly, at us.

PLAUSIBILITY

Just suppose there wasn't a story to occupy your mind
      and your thoughts were free of drama and disdain
you let it all go and only serenity
          controls your heart beat.

Suppose you were content with your life and grateful for what you have
      as if there was nothing lacking in your existence or your livelihood
the inner dreams of your consciousness
          pulsed vibrantly through your veins.

Suppose there is a deeper meaning in your life which allows your mind
      to rest peacefully, when you discover a much higher purpose
on this earth, to nurture and fulfill whatever you focus on, or
          give meaning to, and becomes your true reality.

So just suppose your soul is screaming at you, to simply
      change your perspective, to imagine this is possible
to believe you could swiftly alter your own destiny, what if this once
          you just brazenly embrace something totally new.

What if this once, you just suppose.

TSUNAMI

How latent you lay, waiting for fierce movement deep down under
from an obscure evolving wake. Scientists watch you closely,
literally, your every move, as they chart your data.

But no one knows, not even you, when the earth will shift abruptly
reality will change sequentially for all those who are near
and far, your power fixed in violent motion.

Awakened from your serene and peaceful state.
The mystery that we witness
early morn to evening sun.

The life cycle of our heavenly earth.
Our Mother to whom we honor
encompass and confer.

Yet in our own sea of evolution
tides that rise and fall, within
still, one celestial body.

Tsunami.

STATE OF BEING

Falling into nothingness
is a very slow dive.
        It doesn't talk to you
        straight on.
Nothingness only whispers
to steal your gifts.
        Smothers the loving voice
        inside.

Creeps, shuffles, breathes
rapt, then flips its fin.
        Stupefies, insensible
        then flies.
Out of bold resonance, to soar
loud, clear, deep, strong.
        Reach, divert, transcend
        the fumbled, muddled haze.

THE DICTATED LIFE

Deepak Chopra believes 'you can change your destiny
by the choices you make.' I think he's right about that.
However, there is a dictated life that occurs most undocumented.

Your look, your beauty or lack there of. Your gender, health, build and money,
your family, and what they believe and what they did or did not bestow
upon you.

Your country, city, ethnic neighborhood, your elementary school, middle school,
high school, your community college and all the people within those walls,

whom you so courageously laid your heart out to.
And then, of course, there is your DNA, but don't be fooled by this.
This too can be changed, as fluently as writing it down on a café napkin.

Deepak believes 'you can change your destiny
by the choices you make.' Regardless of everything else,
this is one thing you could do, to step outside of the dictated life.

You could believe, that you can.

ANTIQUATED

Like a bright blue Delphinium, she slowly withers
            dry, grey and white.
Looking, looking for the youth on the outside
                that still breathes on the inside.
She remembers loss and anger, now welcomes
            gratitude, feeling love, softness.
Letting go of old ideas, old expectations even
                older sorrows that no longer wane.

Like a bright blue Delphinium, she salutes the sun
            sways in the wind, spilling fun, joy.
Watches her tawny hair turn brilliant silver, left to toss
                and bobble, eyes smiling in tandem.
All of the memories seem to make more sense.
            All the worries were whispered again then lost.
Adapting like a ravenous Humming Bird, reaching
                through nature, to honor the day.

 One more day.

THE WILD LIFE

The warm weather softly soothes my body and soul
I can sense my pulse release as I gaze out over the water.
The shade of the evergreen trees envelope this little house
and without thinking I take a deep breath, then let it out slow.

If I don't embrace this, I will never really see, or feel it, this
is a very different life. People love it here, hold tight to it.
But unless I go and do it, this will constantly elude me, mess
with my wandering brain and be always just out of reach.

The Madrone trees' red bark is bright and golden as the sun sets on the bay.
It is so beautiful here and unbelievably serene. Occasionally, a trail of cars
go by, to catch the ferry down the road or return to Ganges after being
'off island'. Yet, I'm not bothered by this, watching is remotely entertaining.

I've noticed the people who live here drive slower. It's only the new-comers
who are in some kind of big hurry. I wonder, 'Going somewhere? It's an
island folks! If you drive too fast you will miss the whole experience.'
You'll miss these funny, happy-go-lucky people. You'll miss the wild life.

I plan to breathe it in, let it permeate my whole body, mind and emotions.
I'll take a look ahead, fast forward a bit, ask myself where I want to be
and devise a plan. No rigid choices anymore, only peaceful ones. I love that.
I love that we have a choice. Now that's warm weather in the Canadian Gulf.

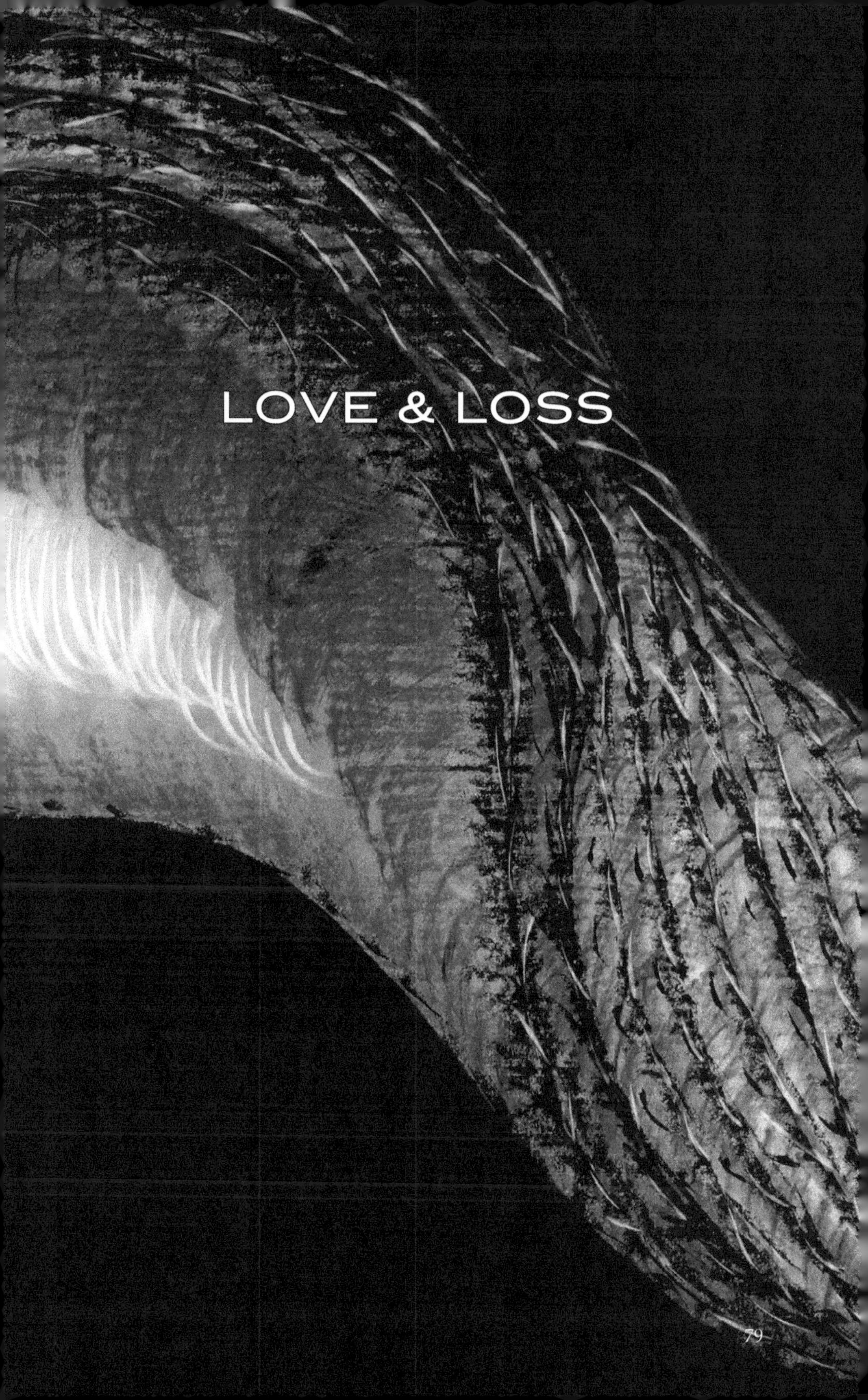

LOVE & LOSS

PASSPORT TO YOUR OWN HEART

If your heart is lost, go buy a new passport
stop intimidating yourself and others with idle
chit-chat and kvetching.
Get on a plane all by yourself and fly to another continent.

Think of your heart as a European country map
open it up and rediscover its true and auspicious beauty
find exciting new places that you have never been within yourself.
Take a train somewhere, anywhere rich with life, colorful, peaceful, quiet.

Then let the fresh air, the vastness, and the loveliness of such a place
feed your soul.
Let it come into your heart and cling to the inner walls of your being
as if it were the intricate painted ceiling of a massive, breath-taking cathedral.

Safe and secure, protected for centuries
or until the need arises, to buy another new passport,
as a cunningly outrageous, and adventurous journey.
As a passport, to your own heart.

THE SHARPENED RIM

Their union was like a broken mirror on any given day
an illness of heart that lay puddled from the constant rain
no justice ensued with a daily emotional mountain eruption.
       Even old literature on the battle of relationships
       waver and dodge the politics of healing, however,
       the art of compassion still flooded in like citrus perfume.

Their love smoldered, heated slowly and then exploded
once again into the hot percolating fire of love consommé,
happiness ran the entire gambit of a raucous football field.
       Boxed-in hatred slid away like sticky, gritty dried up mud
       their separation split open by a numb and dull can opener
       of worms, finally washed clean, in this moment, on this day.

Shining now, like the sharpened rim of a transparent bezel.

BY WAY OF FATE

The first one might have been my greatest lover ever, and
for many years it seemed as though it was true,
but fate took its turn.

The second one, was the one I will never forget. So deep in love
I couldn't see the adulteress, lurking within the misty forest,
who stole the love of my young life.

I was left quietly gasping for air like a crushed grasshopper on the side
of the road. Just a shell, lying there, squished flat. I thought I might die,
really, I assumed my life was over.

The adulteress was my best friend, only I didn't know at the time
she was the other woman. Ironically, after the affair, she invited me
into her home, fed me and nursed me back.

But when she left for Hawaii, to be with this lost love of mine, it finally
occurred to me, she was the one. Right before my eyes,
discreetly behind my back, no explanation.

Deception strikes in many different forms. However, it seems karma
kicked their butts a few weeks later, when their relationship,
truth be told, crumbled.

For me, forgiveness was a winding road that I cautiously navigated
toward success. The first one might have been my greatest lover,
but it is the second one, I will never forget.

FORGIVENESS AND ALL THAT

Forgiveness, smidgness
>
> I told you before, yes, yes I forgive you
>
> I forgave you long ago, forty years in fact
>
> I wish you well, only the best of life.

So please just leave it at that.

Forgiveness, belibness
>
> I can't say it again, I can't relive it either
>
> what's done is done. We all must move on
>
> but I won't choose your devious behavior.

My shrink says I'm better than that.

Forgiveness, morrigness
>
> Take hold of yourself, find what is true
>
> this world trudges on, out of control
>
> discover simplicity, dig in your heels.

All loveliness will bring us right back to that.

GO SWIFT THE BODY'S GUEST

Have you a visitor within your body
       that soothes the bad and celebrates the good
       talks you through a heartfelt cry, a sadness deep.

Does this guest come and go, kick a foot to linger
       clouds your wonder upon early morning rising
       decides in advance whether to survive or pray.

What softness stirs your heart to tears
       conjured by the constant beating
       held to the core of dark defeat.

Yet fills your life…
       with love.

TO SLEEP FOREVER

While driving the Oregon Coast we decided to stop at the Cape
to enjoy the fantastic view and breathe salty sea air
such a stunning, beautiful and powerful place.

We carefully hike the trails along the coastal over hang
stood at the lookout, hugged and shared a kiss
a lovely day, no hurry, just meandering.

When it was time to leave we were walking back in the trees
my love took the high trail and I decided to take the low
but just as I was skipping down to the Manzanitas.

Something stopped me cold, a feeling of doom, and danger
the most horrific energy, daunting, with a loud message
'Don't go down there!', so I turned and headed up.

Two days later on the news we heard about a couple of
passionate teenagers who had been found dead
in the red Manzanita bushes at the Cape.

They were so young and deeply in love, yet
a suicide, an overdose, together in a lovers' pact
forbidden love by societal wrath pushed them into eternity.

Together, alone in the Manzanita bushes on top of Cape Perpetua
above the sea, among the trees, lying down in embrace for the last time.
I sensed their obscure ending, but that sad day, I had no idea it was them.

FREEZING RAIN COLD

She was frozen in life, rigid in love
        in retrogression.

Always gazing to the window
        and stormy skies.

Often screaming at night for the
        fire to reignite.

Lost to the warm weathering
        gift of forgiveness.

Freezing rain cold, icicles
        pierce deep the intricate lining.

Of her delicate, saccharine, yet arctic heart.

COOKIE-LIKE DREAM

I moved the cord and tied the rope.
I imagined that I walked and talked in your cookie-like dream.
There was an office, a basement and pictures of the mountain road
where we first met. There was hope in my heart and singing
                    through the trees.

Your forehead was wrinkled and you were about to cry.
I drove as fast as I could and then I ran the rest of the way.
Up to that mountain, wearing a suit and believing I would see the light
only to learn that your lips were making kissing sounds in the ear
                    of another.

I decided to wake and dream a different day.
I went to the kitchen for coffee and then out into the yard
to eliminate unwanted shoes, rugs and other obscure belongings.
I stopped thinking and hoping, then I drove away in an old tank truck
                    that pulled a trailer.

Presently, I sit in a chair, hitting the wall as I rock.
I want to make a new life.
I feel my time
is now.

ALL I COULD EMBRACE

Soft grains of sand beneath our feet
our hands clasped. My heart soared
in a peaceful existence I had never
       known before.

In my youth I did not know what love was
it escaped me, heart and soul. I thought I knew,
though not until a solemn life on a remote island
did I begin to actually feel it and understand what
       love could be.

So fluid and true that it pulsed in my veins
morning till night. So vast and encompassing
I saw no other faces or heard no conversations.
Walking in the woods together
       was all I could embrace.

BITTEN

Toxic waste stuck deep in our bones
piercing muscles, tendons, veins.
But we do as they say and shake it off.

Let it go to the toxic waste dump
in the sky, shrouded by sunshine,
turning its tide. Cuz we know

how to do that, we've done it
before, we'll do it again and
again. Being bitten doesn't

have to hang around, clogging
pores, stifling life ambitions.
Scars can heal, bites too.

No matter who instills or
what enfolds, watch for
the silver in the lining.

The brilliant non-toxic stuff
remember that's what
beauty is made of.

Wrapped in intimacy and
courage to stand above
for the right to be.

To be who we are.
To do what we love,
no matter how many

times, we might get bitten.

ALOFT AT WAIMEA

The Grand Canyon of the Pacific Ocean
falls deep, brave and strong on Kauai Island
I still see that young woman standing there astonished
Coconut Mai Tai in hand, handsome young love close by.

She was happier there, than ever before, or so she imagined
however short lived, a life sifting through her fingers
like white sand, salty emerald sea in the distance.
Aloft at Waimea, even today, many years later.

The sight of this earthly, vast expanse transforms
her heart falters, skips as she returns swiftly to that day.
Just as if she is there, a summer goddess, on that paradise bluff.
Soft warm wind in her wavy golden hair, she's still standing there.

She's right there. Aloft, at Waimea.

NO LONGER A SAFE HAVEN

How many tender hearts did you break
        how many times was your own heart broken
        unable to comprehend what true love really means.
Your uneducated guess, lost in an obvious display of deception.

There was the faint of heart and the laughing heart wide open
        times of great joy, diving unknowingly right into deep despair
        changes like the wind, set off course by the fierce jet stream array.
Life would pass by so quick, your brain waves would suddenly spin.

The face in the mirror, no longer your own, tentative
        tired eyes telling the long encapsulating story, contiguous
        how many tender hearts were broken, how much left unsaid, unspoken.
No longer a safe haven. But standing stark and alone on that traveling, dreary

Tortuous, sea worthy shore.

THE WIGGLE OF THE FEALTY

You shall wiggle in your fealty, from time to time
without even knowing, the day will come
eyes will bulge, heart to churn, unaware
your loyalty wanes.

You shall wiggle in your fealty, all you thought was so, is not
what you knew to be true, is no longer, reproach, rebuke
and scold yourself to death, the musty
scent of fervor.

You shall wiggle in your fealty, misery fraught with passion
the gaze espies and discerns, love bites sour testimony
redolent, fetid, transported, lost in a constant
revolving, fitful day of dreams.

IMPROMPTU

What is it about this love
        so deep I cannot climb out
        so vast I see the stars escape,
surrounded by laughter and tears.

Warm hugs of the familiar
        never planned or a foreseen future
        love just rolled out its thunder,
without anticipation.

Yet to write it in gracious poetry
        would drown the echo of the
        impromptu evening poem,
as heavy eyes turn to sleep.

For Franzili.

LIFE & DEATH

LAND OF SPIRITS

We live at the east end of town
      just before the landscape mutates
      from small farms to the sultry high desert.
When we drive into the city
      we always pass by the Cemetery
      and refer to it as the 'Land of Spirits'.
We wonder if all those spirits longed
      for their youth with timeless wonderful
      things to accomplish in their earthly lives.

Our days are sometimes like softened clouds
      whispers of gray overhead, polar vortex
      winds, so strong the birds can't fly or breathe.
Heavy like rushing water up their beaks
      yet they hop and jolt from one limb to the
      other. Like us, heads down, contemplating weather.
However, the 'Land of Spirits' uniquely reminds us
      time is of great importance, wrapped everyday
      with new revelations. As we meditate, dream and imagine.

Grateful to be singing on our way,
      for our earthly end has not yet come.

A CURIOUS JOURNEY

She waited till the early morning light,
  after her son had said one last goodbye.
The sheen of the alpine glow shown on her face
  as it softly filtered through her bedroom window.
All her neighbors in the resting graves next door
  waited alert as well, upright in their spirit soup.
No sounds except the wind through the juniper tree
  and the song of the wild bird chirping.

She slipped away peacefully with a quiet pose.
  Brain still sharp with humor intact, yet her
carapace body arranged its slight existence,
  releasing the past for what lay ahead.
Sweet on a Sunday, with patience all week long.
  Giving rise to the way home, one moment at a time.
Love on her shoulder for all to lean, we knew
  how stunning her gifts, how clever her intellect.

We felt the global beating of her sweeping heart.
  They say she waited till the early morning light
to leave this universal, sweet ethereal life
  on a curious journey, no schisms, no strife.

In Memory of Joyce Scott, Proprietor of the Curiosity Shoppe, Bend, Oregon

DEEPLY KEPT

Author Samuel Sagan writes; 'death is the great journey'.

And not to fear, but to welcome the adventure that leads us to it, so
each day has true meaning, as every nuance of life resonates in our soul.

When a complicated heart seeks to be quieted by a warm breeze,
or the fulfillment of a simple day, gently glides into the next.

Time moving beyond what we thought we might miss out on,
forgetting that sometimes doing nothing, ushers us into actual bliss.

How profound just sitting next to the river, awake to the water flow,
such contentment when we experience the certainty of internal peace.

It's deeply kept. This journey, this life, this death.

INDIGO BLUE

An impressive cloud bank a few hundred miles out to sea.
Creeping puffs of gray float slowly toward the sandy shore.
Teenage girls are splashing the surf. Laughing, jumping, running.
Pleasant to watch, but I don't ponder my youth, don't miss it.
What I miss is my brother who died. I've kept it sorely held tight
in my broken pounding heart, but today it comes out, untethered.

Unstoppable. Deep combusting, weeping, mournful tears.
Some days when life was intensely challenging or harsh
the phone would ring, and that laughing voice echoed through.
An immediate soulful link to the loving kindred spirit he was.
Today might be one of those days when he seeks to connect
our spirits once again, by way of the heavenly cosmos.

Filtering down from the billowing cobalt sky above. He would softly
yet seriously remind me to never give up on my dreams. He always
knew how to set me abruptly clear in my thinking, like brothers do.
I imagine he is trolling by, on the just off shore, bobbing fishing vessel,
breathing again, full in, the salty sea air. Loving his favorite place on earth.
On the boat, on the water and on the lapping, quaking waves of Indigo Blue.

THE SPIRAL

There is a path
that sometimes will turn
      inside out and upside down.

The path remains untold to us
we think we know, but we don't
      we hope to go further into the realm.

Of life, not darkness. Of love, not hate.
Then terror ensues, anger cast over peace
      lives are cut from their primordial path.

But 'there is a path' we cry, 'there is a path'.
The path that was given at birth to honor
      until, a horrific kind of blood was spilled.

In our minds, we quake, quiver and pray
in our hearts such deepened sorrow.
      'There was a path', we shout, implore.

And we solemnly tried to follow.

NO REASON

eyes soaked in tears
grey skin encircles
a sea of green

no rest, no sleep
just watching, looking

nose swollen and sore
redness clings to
roughened edges

no joy, no hope
just pain

mouth still, rubs
together, lips of sorrow
silence hangs from thin stature

no reason, no comprehension
just death... her child is gone.

SUDDEN

Zipping bees, pungent earth
in the garden, what wakes
burst free from slumber.

Overnight, buds appear
with gentle, trickling rain
Robins pecking in the grass.

Grouse have ventured in
the male watches sentinel
as the female quietly eats.

The softness of new life
plants and animals
a reticent pause.

To see the world as
not so harsh, fearful
like the daily news.

Here, I can breathe
without the gasp
of sudden useless death.

COOL COTTON

They didn't die, but
thought they should have
      a part of them, terribly aloof, lost
      in thought and moving clouds.

They could only look to the sky
turn their face to the sun, in hope
      of solace there, stone like, remote
      each an invisible, cast bound soul.

Forgiveness opened up, years
months, days, it came and went
      to hover, cry, laugh, love, sleep
      and quietly retreat in sore emotion.

Yet there it was, like pure, ripe fruit
hanging on a tree, bright colors, sweet
      smells, juicy nectars of strife
      always a choice, to either dwell

In the evil thrust upon them
or dwell in the joy of a rich, loving
      surprising life. One where souls don't
      die, and grief is wrapped in cool cotton.

SO STRONG

Yellow and red blowing through the sky
       a gala of swimming leaves
cool winds from sunny to dark. I walk alone
       and fill the space with contemplation.

What loveliness do we all aspire to gain
       when seeking the same peace and bliss
of flocks of birds and honking geese
       the scurried squirrel, or the sleeping cat.

The earth scent in fierce rich tones
       haunted by Halloween
skeletons and twisted trees, death
       to mark a meditation of loved ones.

Gone to Heaven, to the Divine, gone
       to once was. Tugging memories
of what we did, who we were, and how we
       loved so strong. Now lost, forever.

THE PENTIMENTO OF LIFE AND DEATH

My brother slipped into dreams of long ago
    when we were children playing
        on sandy shores of the Columbia River.

His silver green eyes softly gazed at the water
    as if it were a mystical path to eternity
        created by an 18th Century Master Painter.

Only to be covered by the dark pigment of night,
    as he died quietly, falling into
        the layered pentimento of a masterpiece.

The masterpiece of his own artful,
    humorous, much too short, yet
        bold and magnificent life.

As for me,

I slowly descended down the stairway into the earth
    stepping carefully onto a path that became narrow
        then much darker in the shaded woods.

I continued walking on sandy soil and began to hear
    ocean waves rushing onto the beach in syncopated
        gravel, within the water energy of sounds.

Soon, I could see through the thick trees, the pale white sky,
      in the warming afternoon, enveloped by the
            pentimento of my own life, like that old painting.

Feverishly reaching out to the light, I stepped quickly
      toward a salty sea scent, cool fresh air intensified
            breathing, breathing… soulful, but alive.

IN LIEU OF FLOWERS

In lieu of flowers send money cause of death unknown twenty nine golden tan bright blue eyes stunning stature extremely beautiful loving life at its highest adventurist level with family left reeling for answers and none was given each person heralded their close relationship in so many different scenarios yet not one of them seemed sure why such dangerous endeavors were paramount in ones' life but there that photo said it all with the definite sparkle in the eyes a sweet side smile of total happiness soulful understandings a soft yet strong demeanor no question of what exciting new avenue of direction tomorrow would bring no question that life is wonderful and filled with challenges obscure destinations no question that the world the entire planet was a constant playground laid out like a King's feast directly in front of such a mysterious magnetic unforgettable person.

In lieu of flowers... please, send money.

ART & SOUL

WORKS ON PAPER

Beyond all constraints resides an artist
waiting to transport from the everyday.
> Into the view of passion discerning
> what is optical to resonate
> soaked within the physical skin
> observed, unbound, brave.

There are no invented interpretations
for what percolates in the soul.
> Whether it be written word,
> works on paper, paint on canvas
> ink scratched into cold pressed
> textured cloth, or sticky book-glue.

The artist will build a vision
seen or heard or lived.
> Scraping back layers of rich pigment
> humming into hours of quiet contemplation
> resting only when the essence of the memory
> has been effectively played.

DOUBLE DECEPTION

So blatant yet gracefully washed over
    whether written in the 19th, 20th or 21st Century.
The poet has successfully maneuvered evil
    to be hidden within its candor, rhyme or no rhyme.

Not necessarily glossed, the reader still gets a jolt
    of lightning fear and zip-line loathing.
But seriously placed thusly, so not to ring
    true one way or the other.

Titled in such a cloak that softness tempers
    the blow, and pity cannot be offered.
Double deception exemplified, woven discreetly
    through the complex, spilling heart of the poet.

SIMMERING

Is it enough to only live on the crusty fringe
not going raw into the treasured psyche
enjoying every day just for what it is
not regurgitating sticky details.

Is it enough to only write what can be swallowed
holding back horrors of the ancient past
diving in just to the surface water
never stirring the mud within.

What could be risked, can't be retrieved
what could be said, can't be unsaid
love and trust, from long ago.
Enough. Let it sink down.

Down to those wallowing depths
slipping and falling backwards
into the milky matter of that
sloppy, simmering abyss.

GENIUS

Some are afraid of their own genius
others prefer to deny it exists
        even so, don't we all have it
        once we allow it to slip.

Roar, spill, or pace
when it calls, after it occurs
        appears, holds strong to your will
        like a hummingbird flutter.

Into a napping brain on an
overcast day, into a tired
        heart sifting through sadness
        into a body aura of being.

When least expected
surprised by its levity
        composed of permanent form or
        trawled by a spiking luminous light.

THE COIL TIGHTENS

Who bolsters me when I feel sad
      unable to write what's in my heart.
Who says 'you can do it' and
      truly believes I can.
Off traveling far to find my sanity
      seeking places that calm the brain.

Carry on, no matter the circumstance
      the need to triumph, to succeed.
Concrete ideas don't always inform
      life isn't either Yin or Yang.
I can search and discover all I like
      but in my belly the coil tightens.

Something lingers in my gut, to call out
      set clear and acknowledge.
Book after book attempts to guide
      so I reach to the marrow, sacrifice.
All that stifles, all that ruins, all that
      interposes within my life.

PROCESSION

Beneath the clouds of early spring
lays the seed to be watered, to be warmed
      then lifted by the energy of a new day
      just like the spirit within a lonely child
      or the dampness of a divided heart.

Waiting for the sun, we know no bounds
wanting to be free of the stuffy smells
      the closed up house, forced air heat
      slowly the jet stream rises, but not soon
      enough, shy to clear the spinning webs.

Of the mind, of the writer's will, as it awakens
to feel the casting sun, no excuses to wither
      even further than winter's sleepy grasp
      rumble the words, express new thoughts
      encompass caprice, a love for the bleeding soul.

AT CANNON BEACH

Stormy days on the coast at Cannon Beach
welcomed there with no shortage of things to do,
even when the rain mingles with the silky Pacific Surf.
On the western edge of North America driftwood scatters
the sand, bright aqua waves crash upon annexed sea stacks,
storms strike the coastline, often with fury, at 50 miles per hour.

Colonies of Cormorants and Seagulls live peacefully together,
as dozens of Pelicans flock boisterously to the mouth of Ecola Creek.
Harbor seals, gray whales and marine mammals are often seen just
off shore, some more curious while others are flippant and evasive.
Through autumn to winter months the Oregon Coast is drenched
with ample traveling precipitation.

Artists bend the lines challenging themselves to escape
the sea salt boredom. They keep the element of mystery in their work
as they draw from imagination. Bicycles fly toward the horizon, huge
apples fall from twisted trees, piano keyboards curve like the frame of
a baby grand. Breathe in the misty coastal journey as life becomes art,
becomes life. Be-cloud the painting, to feel other than the typical,
sorcerous, sleepy mundane.

THE HAUNTING

Paper rules the universe, haunting
        a writer's friend or enemy
laid, carefully arranged, stapled
        bonded, stacked, or crumpled.

Wasted in the waste basket
        recycled, reprinted, reworked, copied
white, red, purple, yellow, green, blue
        all the same in depth and length.

Taking over file cabinets, counter tops,
        storage bins. Lined by subject matter
on the book shelf, hanging in calendar splendor
        and put upon the window pane.

All in a profound need of letting go
        now, more than ever, the old reports, letters
journals from lives past, long gone
        each tossed into the burning cauldron.

Calling up the braver part of a psyche
        to coax the 'must-save-everything' brain
finally freed, current, untethered, clear
        copious space, for better than average, novel ideas.

TRUTH RISING

Write every day, write every morning
early morning, a constant daily ritual to embrace
a dawning spiritual journey through my heart and back again
inspired once more, literally on fire, like the simmering morning sun.

I can hear the intense and endearing words of other writers
souls bleed and with them, mine as well, to try to tell my story too
eager to fill the lake, drifting along the river that empties swift within it
enduring. I feel pain, scream out in the night, or laugh loud
from my spirited belly.

There is an irony that washes over me when I least expect it
the lessons learned, or not learned and the repetition of failure or regrets
how to weave a story of my own liking, my own needs and emotions
the never ending ego of desire. It's all in there. Wrapped up
like Christmas on a cold morning. It's all there.

Waiting for the dam to break, the walls to crumble or the people to die.
Through life, I have been many things, so close to what I thought
I should be, but now it's time to write, early morning, morning ritual.
Sit and just write. I don't need to be anything anymore.
Artist, Painter, Singer, Writer.

No label, of any kind, will ever help me find, my own true soul.

CONSEQUENTLY

On my way here I learned about transforming myself from the darkness
  into the light.
Scratching my way to the surface to create a happy, secure
   and meaningful life.
All the hidden tears I cried over the many years soaked into
   my thirsty heart.
Then spilled like a waterfall to feed the sandy beaches below
    and bled into my soul.

I remember thinking when I was young
  there must be a better way to exist in the world.
Struggling every day to overcome, to strive to be better
  to educate myself and excel.
I wondered about the earth and how it evolves
   how it takes us with it as passengers.
Swirling in deaths' heaviness, as ashes dust our fields
   waterways and our psyches.

I regret only that I rushed through some of the most important times
  significant days.
Allowing myself to push too hard, play too long, or even self-destruct
  my own potential.

However, this much I know, I won't profess enlightenment
for then it will exit my grasp.

Entering Nirvana* can take us serenely on a continuous journey of love
connection and joy.

Consequently… this is enough, for me.

Nirvana* – 'The final freeing of a soul from all that enslaves it.
The supreme happiness that comes when all obsession, hatred
and delusion die out.' 'Buddha'

FULL MOON ON MY SHOULDER

The Harvest Moon, full and striking
                        born to the black night sky
            salty breezes linger from the bay.

The rhapsody of illness and struggle ensued
                        a baby arrives as a family moves away
            no time to bond with the newness of reality.

Born with a Virus, and a quiet whimper
                        placed alone in an incubator, attached
            to hydration, consoled and labeled.

The angel clan assembled, to lift up this little one
                        count the heart beat slow to rhythm
            calling the new born spirit to fight, to live.

Days and weeks of quiet constellation
                        till one day, through cold winter mountains
            the Mother returns to find a life renewed.

This babe, this infant soul, not known
                        sleeps peaceful, yet fierce in resolve
            with the full moon, on my shoulder.

ABOUT THE AUTHOR

Cheri Lee Helfenstein, nee, Cheri Lee Haven was born in Washington State and grew up in the Wenatchee Valley on the Columbia River. She traveled and lived in Alaska for eight years with one year on the Trans-Alaska Pipeline at the Arctic Circle. Cheri Lee is a 2017 Colrain Poetry Manuscript Conference Alumni. In 2012, her poem 'For the Dead Dragonfly' placed as a Winning Entry in the Literary Harvest Poetry Contest with the Central Oregon Writers Guild. Her first book of poems, 'Rock Speaks Loud, Soft yet Strong' was published in 1995. And her poem 'We Both Shall Rise' was published in the 1992 *National Library of Poetry* Book. She's published in several different genres of Poetry Anthologies.

Cheri Lee is also an artist. She graduated Magna Cum Laude with Honors from Southern Oregon University, Ashland, Oregon, with a Bachelor of Arts Degree in Painting and Drawing. She also earned a Chinese Brush Painting Certificate from the University of Oregon, and completed the Art for Teachers Course, at the Oregon State University, Cascade Campus. Cheri Lee taught Painting, Drawing, and Art Portfolio, as well as, Tai Chi Chuan and Qigong for several years at Central Oregon Community College. She has been a Tai Chi and Qigong Practitioner for over 30 years. Cheri Lee is now retired from teaching to focus on her passions of Writing, Painting and Travel. She resides in Bend, Oregon.

Art Website: www.cherilee.com

www.ingramcontent.com/pod-product-compliance
Lightning Source LLC
Chambersburg PA
CBHW071228090426
42736CB00014B/3011